Bu$ine$$ Leader$

RALPH LAUREN

Myra Weatherly

MORGAN
REYNOLDS
PUBLISHING
Greensboro, North Carolina

Bu$ine$$ Leader$:

Russell Simmons
Steve Jobs
Oprah Winfrey
Warren Buffett
Michael Dell
Ralph Lauren
Faces Behind Beauty

BUSINESS LEADERS: RALPH LAUREN

Copyright © 2009 By Myra Weatherly

Library of Congress Cataloging-in-Publication Data

Weatherly, Myra.
  Business leaders : Ralph Lauren / by Myra Weatherly. -- 1st ed.
    p. cm.
  Includes bibliographical references and index.
  ISBN-13: 978-1-59935-084-4
  ISBN-10: 1-59935-084-X
  1. Lauren, Ralph. 2. Fashion designers--United States--Biography. I.
Title.
  TT505.L38W43 2008
  746.9'2092--dc22
  [B]
                                        2008009216

Printed in the United States of America
First Edition

For Justin Owen James

Contents

Ralph Lauren
(Courtesy of AP Images/Dima Gavrysh)

ONE
Childhood Dreams

By the age of three, Ralph Lauren already possessed a definite sense of style. It started with hats. He liked to wear one at all times, just like his grandfather Sam Lifshitz, a devout Jew who fled the pogroms of Russia and immigrated to the United States in 1920, working until his last days as a night watchman and janitor at a New York clothing and linen store. Ralph sported hats that belonged to his father and two older brothers as well, and occasionally he improvised, putting the metal cover of a potato boiler on his head, as if it were a helmet.

In high school, Ralph used earnings from a part-time job to buy high-quality clothing from secondhand stores. He and a buddy would drive into Manhattan, in a 1949 Pontiac owned by Ralph's dad, and search thrift shops for great, cheap clothes. An old pair of army pants, or better yet a bomber jacket, was considered a real find, but it had to look "like it lived."

School mates dubbed him "a dresser," and one friend later recalled that "Ralph would show up in things that were 'off the wall' but always looked great . . . You could try to copy his look but you wouldn't look the way he looked."

Ralph's attraction to clothes and his passion for dressing well mystified his family. In time, however, Ralph Lauren would become one of the world's most successful fashion designers, turning his personal passion for style into a multibillion dollar business whose logo, an equestrian with a polo mallet, would be a top global icon, recognized from America to Tokyo to Russia.

Ralph Lauren was born Ralph Lifshitz on October 14, 1939, in the Bronx, New York City. He was the youngest of four children of Frank and Frieda Lifshitz, first-generation Russian Jewish immigrants. Ralph's sister Thelma, born in 1930, started life during the hard times of the Great Depression. Then came brother Lenny in 1932, followed by Jerry in 1934. In 1939, war clouds loomed over Europe. A few weeks before Ralph's birth on October 14, England and France declared war on Germany, marking the beginning of World War II.

At the time of Ralph's birth, the Lifshitz family lived in a sturdy six-story red brick apartment building in the Mosholu Parkway section of the Bronx. Surrounded by parks, this treelined neighborhood was home to first and second generation Jews, Italians, and Irish. It was a neighborhood of shopkeepers, garment workers, and furriers. Most parents spoke broken English. They hoped and dreamed of their children becoming doctors, lawyers, or owning successful businesses.

A view of a street in the Bronx in 1955 *(Courtesy of FPG/Getty Images)*

Ralph and his older brothers shared a bedroom that over-looked the school yard of Public School 80. The second bedroom belonged to Frieda and Frank. Thelma slept on a pull-out sofa in the living room. As the youngest boy, Ralph inherited his brother's hand-me-downs.

"The clothes went from Lenny to Jerry to me. I guess it was important to have new things, but some of those clothes, I really wanted," Ralph later recalled. "As a kid, I was always into clothes, but I didn't have the money to buy them." What he did have, however, was an intense desire to "be rich."

Like other residents in the Bronx neighborhood, the Lifshitz family struggled to get by. Serious-minded and religious, Frieda Lifshitz reared her children in the Jewish faith and instilled in them a strong sense of family values. Frank Lifshitz painted houses and apartments to support his family. But he dreamed of becoming an artist, and murals that he created in the lobbies of New York office buildings brought him great satisfaction.

Growing up, Ralph idolized baseball greats Mickey Mantle, Joe DiMaggio, and other sports legends, and even dreamed of a becoming a professional athlete himself. He also loved movies, especially westerns and the cowboy actor, Randolph Scott. Much later, the Wild West look would influence his designs in clothing and home furnishings.

Ralph's mother wanted him to become a rabbi, and he attended mostly private Jewish schools until the end of his freshman year in high school. Then he switched to a public school, DeWitt Clinton, an all-boys' high school. Although he tried out for the basketball team at DeWitt Clinton every year, Ralph never made the team. In a school with 4,000 students, it proved impossible for him to break in. Nonetheless, Ralph found a way to stand out among his peers. He developed a reputation as a trendy dresser.

"I was not a kid who walked around all day in beautiful clothes and pranced in front of a mirror. I was a very natural kid, did all the things everyone did," Ralph said later. "But I wasn't afraid of taste. I was not afraid of expressing myself, and a lot of kids were."

Randolph Scott *(Courtesy of Silver Screen Collection/Hulton Archive/Getty Images)*

The entrance to Camp Roosevelt

During the summer months, Ralph worked at Camp Roosevelt in the Catskill Mountains of upstate New York, first as a waiter and eventually as a camp counselor. "A waiter was the lowlife at the camp," said Ralph. "You're working, the rich kids are the campers, and you'd only get to go on the basketball courts when the kids or the counselors were gone." Becoming a counselor was a high point for Ralph. "I started nowhere, at the bottom . . . and I worked my way up to being top counselor. It sounds like nothing now, but at the time it was very important to me."

The three summers spent at Camp Roosevelt opened up a whole new world of sophistication for Ralph—a world beyond the close-knit immigrant community of his parents.

He saw how people with money lived, and he connected with their attitudes, values, and particularly their way of dressing.

During his last summer at Camp Roosevelt, Ralph decided to change his surname from Lifshitz to Lauren; his given name has a four-letter word in it that neighborhood kids used to tease him about. "Kids would laugh," he said. "In class, every time I got up it would make me sweat. A little kid with a funny name." His brother Jerry changed his name to Lauren also, but the rest of the family kept the name Lifshitz, as it connected them to their Jewish European heritage.

In 1957, Ralph graduated from DeWitt Clinton High School. Beneath his senior picture in the yearbook, he listed his ambition: millionaire.

TWO

A Passion for Clothes

After graduation from high school, Lauren enrolled at the City College of New York (CCNY). Located at Lexington Avenue and Twenty-third Street, CCNY was a long commute from the Bronx, where Lauren still lived with his family, and a long way from the preppy dreams of college inspired by Camp Roosevelt.

At first, Lauren attended day classes, studying business. Then, he switched to night classes so he could get a job. He found work at Allied Stores, a department store buying office. Store employees, known as buyers, combed the streets of Manhattan's garment district, ordering clothing for retail stores. Lauren's job was to log returned merchandise. Mundane as the job was, the salary of fifty dollars a week was enough to buy clothes and to take girls out on dates.

In the beginning, Lauren enjoyed the business world. Yet the more he saw of Allied Stores, the more disenchanted he became. He said, "A lot of people I met in business did not have integrity. They were not honest."

In time, Lauren became just as disillusioned with the university, and quit in his third year. "It was tough on my family. Everyone went to college, and I was the one that did not make it." Though he missed having "a really great education," Lauren said, "I was so busy trying to become something . . . that I had to work."

Finding work in the summer of 1960 was far from easy. Now that Lauren had dropped out of college, he was eligible for the armed forces draft, and "nobody would hire you until you got the service out of the way," he recalled.

His older brother Jerry stepped in to help his younger brother. Thinking that maybe Ralph should be selling clothes instead of buying them, he called a college friend, Neal Fox, who worked at Brooks Brothers. Founded in 1818, the first Brooks Brothers opened in Lower Manhattan, where the South Street Seaport now stands. It was one of the first stores in the United States to carry ready-to-wear suits in addition to hand-tailored suits. Throughout its long history, Brooks Brothers has had a long list of distinguished clientele, including President Abraham Lincoln, England's Duke of Windsor, and author F. Scott Fitzgerald. In the late 1950s, prep school students and members of high society shopped there—the very world that appealed to Ralph Lauren.

With a personal recommendation from Fox, Brooks Brothers hired Lauren, and he started out as a salesman at Brook's Madison Avenue store. "[Ralph] was responsible for the neckwear," recalled Joe Barrato, then manager of the Brooks custom suit department. "When he finished sorting

Customers shopping inside a Brooks Brothers store in 1954. *(Courtesy of Nina Leen/Time Life Pictures/Getty Images)*

ties, they looked like soldiers at attention, so beautiful, so I asked who did that. That's how we met. We bonded."

Working at Brooks Brothers, while waiting to be drafted, gave Lauren even more exposure to the upper-middle class. He saw that the customers expected personal service—and they did not mind paying for it.

Then, on December 30, 1960, Lauren received his draft notice. Three months later, he left Brooks Brothers and shipped out to Fort Dix in central New Jersey for basic training in the U.S. Army Reserves. Upon arriving at the induction center, he witnessed the hazing of a fellow inductee named Lifshitz. Lauren was glad he had changed his name.

Not surprisingly, army life did not appeal to Lauren. "You have no face, you're not a person, you're a robot," he said. But he did like the uniform, "I wear khaki, I love army clothes." Handing out uniforms to other soldiers was a part of his job as supply clerk. He served six months at Fort Dix and remained on call in an Army Reserve Contingency Group for another fifteen months.

After Fort Dix, twenty-two-year-old Lauren moved back into his childhood bedroom. He landed his first full-time permanent job as shipping clerk at Meyers Make, a manufacturer of gloves. "My job was to take the order books of the salesmen, check the number of orders and when they were to be shipped, and then mail them," he recalled. Posting orders bored him, but he did not quit. Before long, he joined the sales force, pounding the pavement, going door-to-door to clothing stores with his box of gloves. "Basically, I was selling women's gloves that buttoned up to the elbow," he said. "Then I'd sit in on the sales meetings, with some real old-timers, and I'd learn."

It was a job with no future, however. In the relaxed atmosphere of President John F. Kennedy's administration, items such as men's hats and elbow-length gloves were on their way out of fashion.

Meyers Make of New York eventually went out of business, but before it closed, Ed Brandau, a friend from Brooks Brothers, offered Lauren a job. Brandau was head of sales at glove-maker Daniel Hays. He told Lauren that the company had outfitted Theodore Roosevelt's Roughriders during the Spanish American War and now made seamless gloves that fit "like the skin on your hand." Lauren took the job in the summer of 1963. To supplement his meager salary, Lauren soon began selling perfume also. The scent he sold was Zizanie. Created in 1932 by French perfumer Fragonard, Zizanie is still available for purchase.

Lauren was good at his job and buyers liked his style. But Brandau said, "He had a tendency to be a dreamer. He wasn't really . . . well, how interested in gloves could you be? He was always dreaming of the future and what he could do."

One new account did get Lauren excited. He bounded into Brandau's office to tell him he had just opened an account selling gloves to an equestrian shop on Madison Avenue. The store specialized in riding clothes and polo gear. Brandau remembered Ralph's fascination with the store's clientele. "He liked the lifestyle. You could see he wanted all those things."

Anything English impressed Lauren. Stretching his modest earnings, he purchased a Morgan, an English sports car. The Morgan line launched in 1909. The cars are sleek and fast, and Lauren loved his two-seater.

Needing more money to support his increasingly expensive tastes, Lauren took a better paying job in 1964 as the

A Morgan sports car on display at an auto show

New York sales representative for A. Rivetz & Company, a tie-maker based in Boston. Rivetz sold conservative ties to stores such as Brooks Brothers, Bloomingdale's, and men's wear specialty shops. Lauren handled all of the company's accounts in the Long Island area. At that time, the tie industry stayed basically the same year after year. Consistency was a virtue. If change ever occurred, it was a slight variation in the dyeing process. Ties remained thin.

While the other salesmen in the company dressed to fit in, Lauren dressed to make a bold statement. "He pulls up in a Morgan wearing a World War II leather aviator's jacket, a leather aviator's hat with goggles," said Robert Stack, a salesman at one of Ralph's Rivetz accounts. Instead of a tie salesman, Stack thought he "looked like somebody from outer space."

Although Lauren, twenty years younger than any other salesman, baffled his co-workers, people outside the office took notice of him. On May 21, 1964, a full page devoted to Ralph Lauren's wardrobe appeared in *Daily News Record*, the men's wear industry newspaper. Titled "The Professional Touch," the piece included sketches and detailed descriptions of some of Lauren's unique outfits. The article described Lauren's clothes as "a season's jump ahead of the market." All the attention heaped upon the new kid stunned his co-workers at Rivetz—but not his boss.

Abe Rivetz liked Lauren and recognized his talent. He even began going to Lauren's tailor. "Abe understood me," said Lauren. "He had that little extra, that hunger . . . We were close."

Despite their closeness, Rivetz disliked Lauren's cream-colored Morgan. It had a sporty red leather interior but lacked a trunk. Lauren drove around with the sample ties in a little space behind the front seat, clearly visible through the car windows. "Somebody will steal our line," predicted Abe Rivetz. "Get rid of it. Get a salesman's car, a car with a trunk that locks."

To show loyalty to the company, Lauren gave in and sold his Morgan. But instead of buying a car similar to ones driven by the other salesmen, Lauren's next car was a sporty 1957 Ford Thunderbird.

A few months before joining Rivetz, Lauren had met Ricky Low-Beer, a part-time receptionist at his eye doctor's office. Ricky was six years younger than Lauren and quite beautiful. Later Lauren insisted it was love at first sight. "She was very European," Lauren said. "She was an only child and very sheltered; she had never even had an ice-cream soda until I met her . . . She was unlike any American girl I'd seen." This stunning blonde with pale blue eyes and trim figure was an English major at Hunter College in New York City. She also taught dance part-time at a Fred Astaire studio. Some of the couple's earliest dates were spent at a club in the Gotham Hotel. Lauren remembers the club as being "European, the Beatles were happening . . . It was chic, and very, very glamorous."

Lauren's style of dressing impressed Ricky. She said, "He actually dressed like my relatives who were European."

Although there were differences in their backgrounds, Lauren and Ricky had a lot in common. Both were children of first-generation immigrants. Ricky's parents came from Austria. Her father Rudolph descended from a long line of prominent Jews in Germany, but he married outside the faith: Ricky's mother was a Catholic. Like Lauren, Ricky had a direct link to the Holocaust generation. Her parents fled Vienna just before World War II at the time Adolf Hitler came to power in Germany. They settled in Shanghai. The Chinese city became home to thousands of Jews fleeing the Nazi threat in Europe. Ricky's parents left Shanghai for the U.S. before the Japanese forced the Shanghai Jews into a ghetto in 1942. A few years later, on January 21, 1945, Ricky Low-Beer was born. But she was not born Jewish: according to Jewish law, Judaism is passed down through the female side of the family. Lauren told some of his friends that Ricky was not Jewish, but he did not want his parents to know.

On December 20, 1964, Lauren and Ricky were married at Burnside Manor in the Bronx. Longtime friend Steve Bell served as Lauren's best man. After the wedding, Jeb Buchwald drove the couple to the airport.

Lauren and his wife, Ricky, in 1997. *(Courtesy of AP Images/Don Pollard)*

When they returned from their honeymoon, they moved into their first home—a one-bedroom apartment with a kitchen in the living room. Ricky remembers their first home as a place of great happiness. Because they were short on money, the newlyweds shopped in thrift shops, trying to bring a bohemian look to their new home. The apartment, located on Knox Place, was a few blocks from Lauren's parents' house.

Lauren continued to work for Rivetz, and his bride returned to college, preparing to become an elementary school teacher.

THREE

The Wide Tie

Abe Rivetz died on the day Ralph Lauren and Ricky Low-Beer married. Mel Creedman, Rivetz's son-in-law, quickly took over the business. Abe Rivetz had believed in Lauren, offering friendship and encouragement. But Creedman thought he was an amateur and immature. Lauren's new boss declared, "The world is not ready for Ralph Lauren."

In the early 1960s, men's ties were dark and narrow and stayed the same shape and width from year to year. Even so, Lauren pressured his new boss with the idea of designing a modern tie for Rivetz to carry, similar to the wide flamboyant ties worn by young European men, especially rock stars. He envisioned his wide ties in vibrant colors. They would make a new fashion statement and appeal to a broad range of men. Creedman, who had no faith in Lauren, refused. He said, "There's no such thing as a designer in our business."

Lauren taken in 1965. *(Courtesy of Jack Robinson/Hulton Archive/Getty Images)*

A 1960 photo of a suit and narrow tie *(Courtesy of Nat Farbman/Time Life Pictures/Getty Images)*

Creedman thought Lauren should spend more time selling ties and less time talking fashion.

Since he would not be designing ties for A. Rivetz & Co., Lauren began searching for a new job. He aspired to launch his own tie company, but he lacked the money to open a business. His parents did not have money to lend him; neither did his brothers. But that did not stop him. Lauren had the full support of his wife Ricky. "I know you have the feeling you can fly. I know you can fly, and I want you to fly," Ricky wrote to Lauren.

During the winter and spring of 1967, Lauren contacted potential financial backers. He shared his enthusiasm and displayed samples of his four-inch-wide neckties. "They were all handmade from old fabrics and little pieces of odds and ends," Lauren recalled.

At the time, ties were inexpensive: three or four dollars each. Lauren wanted to change the prices, too. "The ties I wanted to sell started at seven fifty." On the high end, his ties retailed for $15.00.

But his new and expensive ties were a hard sell. Mel Creedman was not the only person who doubted that the world was ready for Ralph Lauren. Risking their money on a twenty-six-year-old tie salesman was simply not an option for many potential investors. No matter, Lauren continued to make contacts. His break came in April of 1967.

After working four years with A. Rivetz & Co., Lauren finally networked his way into a deal with conservative tie-maker Beau Brummell. Although Lauren's wide ties were the opposite of the Beau Brummell look, company president Ned Brower agreed to manufacture and sell Lauren's ties. He thought the wide tie would be an asset to his already successful company. And if the line failed, his company could easily absorb the losses.

Now that he had his own line, Lauren needed a name that was both sporty and elegant. "I could not call it basketball or baseball," Lauren said. After tossing around many names associated with sports, he settled on Polo. The name proved to be a masterstroke: polo is a game played by the wealthy and aristocratic, people like Prince Charles of England. Polo

A 1940s etching of polo players on the field *(Library of Congress)*

conveys the same qualities that Lauren wanted for his ties—
money and style. It had "an international quality, a sense of
Europe . . . [It] was sports mixed with style and lifestyle . .
." Even today, forty years later, Polo signifies the distinction
that Lauren intended his product to have.

Lauren's division was a one-man operation. As the only
employee, he designed the ties, purchased materials, and super-
vised the manufacturing. His responsibilities also included
packing and shipping the orders as well as keeping financial records. He did it all from Beau Brummell's New York
offices in the Empire State Building. "They gave me a tiny
office and I kept my ties in a drawer," Lauren said.

Lauren was happy to be designing the kinds of ties he had always dreamed of creating. He rummaged the remnant shops that lined the Lower East Side of Manhattan for unique fabrics. He bought hand-blocked prints in bright colors, diagonal checks, and attention-getting exotic materials.

Arms loaded with fabrics, Lauren arrived at the workroom of George Bruder, a highly respected tie-maker of the day. He showed Bruder the fabrics and his ideas for the new line and asked if he could make the ties to his specific directions. Bruder, who had made Lauren's first ties, agreed. Lauren ordered only two dozen ties at the time. "I couldn't make any money on orders that small, but I liked Lauren, so I did it. You needed a lot of patience to work with him, too, because on top of everything else he would sit there and actually quibble over one-sixteenth of an inch," Bruder recalled. Each of Lauren's ties was hand slip-stitched in such a way that they retained their fat bottle shape, even when tugged. It took longer to make ties using this method and it cost more. But since Lauren never shied away from an expensive wardrobe for himself, he assumed his customers would not either.

Lauren had definite ideas about the kind of stores he wanted to carry his ties. He selected the top specialty men's wear stores to visit and show his line. In August 1967, Lauren told a reporter, "The store gives the tie the right or wrong connotations. I want a few good stores, not the commercial market . . . I'm promoting a level of taste, a total feeling." Increasingly, fellow salesmen and tailors liked his ties—but retailers were nervous. Many buyers who liked the look were turned off by the price. They complained that customers would not pay so much. However, some stores started stocking the ties.

Lauren sold his ties to Paul Stuart, the store where he bought many of his own clothes. The Paul Stuart name gave him bragging rights and impressed other customers. The same was true at Meledandri, another exclusive men's store. They did not place big orders, but just having his ties in those stores helped Lauren sell to other stores.

Lauren's strategy worked. Small stores outside of New York City began selling his ties. One client, Louis of Boston, catered to wealthy customers. Berny Schwartz stocked Polo ties in his Eric Ross men's store in Beverly Hills, California. "Wearing a Ralph Lauren tie in those days was like belonging to a fraternity," Schwartz said. "No matter who you saw and where you saw them, you were identified as a fraternity brother. It could be on a plane, in an elevator, but when you saw someone wearing one of his ties, you smiled."

Neiman Marcus, the upscale specialty store in Dallas, Texas, also became a client. On a buying trip to New York, Neal Fox, vice-president of men's and boys' clothing, checked out Lauren's new tie collection. Lauren and Fox were not strangers. Years before, Fox had helped Lauren get his job at Brooks Brothers. Fox liked the collection. "It was fabulous, a breakthrough in shape, fabrication, point of view," he said. Fox urged Lauren to send some swatches down to the company's tie buyer.

Instead of sending samples, Lauren went to Dallas. "At the time, I wasn't big on flying . . . I wasn't that experienced in jetting all over the place," Lauren said. "But I got my little rags [ties] together, got on a plane, and flew there because I knew the buyer wouldn't understand my ties unless I explained them in person." He returned home with an astounding order for one hundred dozen ties.

With this success, Lauren's next goal was to sell his ties to Bloomingdale's—the store in the forefront of fashion. He made his first attempts while working at Rivetz. He learned that their tie buyers relied on long-standing relationships with salesmen. Though not a member of the "club," Lauren had no doubt that sooner or later the prestigious store would want his ties since Bloomingdale's customers were wealthy and sophisticated.

In the meantime, Polo had no money for advertising. So far, Lauren had used word-of-mouth to build his business. What Lauren needed was someone to introduce him to the buyers of big stores, especially Bloomingdale's. He found a champion: Joe Aezen, a salesman for Rooster ties. The two met at a trade show when Lauren worked for the Daniel Hays Company. Aezen was loud and compulsive. He even made up a jingle to help people remember his names: "Aezen as in raisin as in Rooster as in chicken." Despite his zany showmanship, buyers liked him. Aezen was very vocal in his enthusiasm for Lauren's ties. When he made his rounds to stores each week selling Rooster ties, he handed out Polo ties to the buyers and to the assistant buyers. In no way did Lauren's ties compete in style or price with the Rooster line.

Aezen was unrelenting with his sales pitch to the executives at Bloomingdale's. He talked and talked some more about Lauren to Franklin Simon, to Jack Schultz, to Gary Shafer, and to Steve Krauss. Schultz, divisional merchandise manager, remembered that Joe Aezen would take "Frank Simon and me to dinner, or bring us brownies when we worked late, and all the time he'd be telling us that we had to have those Ralph Lauren ties." Finally, as a favor to Aezen, Gary Shafer, the store's tie buyer, made Lauren an offer.

He agreed to buy some Polo ties on two conditions: make the ties narrower and remove the Polo label and replace with Bloomingdale's label. Although selling to Bloomingdale's would have given Lauren an edge and increased his sales, he said no. He told Shafer, "Gary, I'm dying to sell to Bloomingdale's, but I'm closing my bag because I can't take my name off. And I can't make the tie a quarter of an inch narrower." Lauren knew if he watered down his concept, his ties would lose their distinctiveness. He had no doubt that sooner or later Bloomingdale's would buy his ties with the Polo label inside and no change in design.

Ned Brower, owner of Beau Brummell, did not understand Lauren's gutsy move. The fledgling company needed money. In his first six months in business, Lauren opened only two dozen accounts. Even so, he needed more office space. Brower moved Lauren to a slightly larger space in the back half of the company's Empire State Building office. Though still cramped, Lauren had a desk and a chest of drawers. "It was like a prison cell," said Joe Aezen.

From his new office, Lauren continued to drive from account to account, in his latest cream-colored Morgan, hand delivering his ties, sometimes with his wife Ricky, sometimes with George Bruder, his tie-maker. Bruder loved to watch Lauren set up his displays. "I saw a young man who had a fantastic drive, and once he was onto something, wouldn't let go."

Lauren spent hours talking to fashion editors at magazines and newspapers, gaining a lot of press coverage very early. His time and efforts paid off when Robert L. Green, an influential men's fashion editor at *Playboy*, took notice. *Playboy* used Lauren's ties in a feature on men's fashion. Others noticed and Lauren's following grew.

Even so, Ralph Lauren's fixation on Bloomingdale's never wavered. In the spring of 1968, several months after turning down the big store's initial offer, Ralph Lauren's ties were finally stocked in the men's department of Bloomingdale's in Fresh Meadow, a suburb of New York City.

Steve Krauss gave Lauren his big break. Krauss, former assistant tie manager at the flagship store, had been promoted to head the men's department in Bloomingdale's Fresh Meadow store. As a rule, department managers do not do their own buying, but Krauss liked and wanted Lauren's ties. He quietly placed an order. "After we put Lauren's ties in, the business exploded," said Krauss. He found it hard to believe because the "prices were crazy for those days." Unable to ignore the success of the branch store, Bloomingdale's main store in the city soon began stocking Polo ties. Marvin Traub, head of Bloomingdale's, remembered Lauren being ecstatic. Lauren delivered the ties himself, leaving his car parked at the curb, running in dressed in a bomber jacket and jeans. On Saturdays, he was in the store "to straighten his cases. . . He would give demonstrations on how his ties should be knotted, how he wanted them with a dimple, just so."

For Father's Day in 1968, Bloomingdale's Lexington Avenue store set up a special display of Lauren ties. Lauren was so excited that he insisted on polishing the four-foot glass showcase himself. This was the start of a long-term profitable relationship between Lauren and Bloomingdale's.

Having been in business for more than a year, Lauren told a reporter from the *Daily News Record*, "My long-range wish would be to design all kinds of men's wear, not just ties."

FOUR

Founding a Fashion Empire

After being in business with Beau Brummell for a year, Lauren told a friend that his ties were finally working. "All of a sudden the name Polo was hot," he said. However, his backer Ned Brower was less than enthusiastic.

Brower worried about the low volume of ties that Lauren sold. He had never been happy with the excessive amount of money that Lauren spent producing his work, and to Brower, turning down large customers such as Wallach's, a chain of men's stores, and Macy's department store because they did not fit Lauren's image of exclusivity was a serious mistake.

Hearing of Lauren's problems, Joe Aezen, Frank Simon, and Jack Schultz advised him to break away from Beau Brummell and Brower. Schultz of Bloomingdale's said, "Brower didn't get what Lauren was proposing. Lauren was about style, not profit." His business friends pushed him to expand his line. They thought he could do the same thing for suits as he was doing with ties. Lauren thought so, too. But again he lacked the money to expand his business.

A short time later, Norman Hilton, a third-generation suit manufacturer, took notice of Lauren. The Hilton family factory in New Jersey made high-end suits for such fine stores as Brooks Brothers and Saks Fifth Avenue in New York City. Norman Hilton was aggressive and demanding. In the spring of 1968, his instincts told him that something new was on the horizon in men's fashions. All over town, he noticed that "people who were really hip began showing up with beautiful fat ties." Sales reps wore them, buyers wore them, and Bloomingdale's carried them. Hilton said to Peter Strom, his executive vice-president, "Pete, go find out where those ties are coming from. I'm interested. Whoever is making those ties should be making them for Norman Hilton." Strom reported back that the ties were the work of twenty-nine-year-old Ralph Lauren, and the young man had started a fashion revolution that showed no signs of stopping. Hilton promptly called Lauren and arranged a meeting.

When they met, Hilton offered Lauren a job making ties for him. But just as Lauren had told the *Daily News Record,* he wanted to design men's wear in general, not just ties. Also, he wanted his own company. Neither budged and the meeting ended.

That summer, Lauren and Peter Strom developed a close friendship while vacationing at the New York beach community known as the Hamptons. More and more, Strom became fascinated with Lauren and his ideas. By the end of summer, Strom was ready to reopen negotiations with Lauren. Now, he had to convince Hilton.

Encouraged by Strom, Norman Hilton agreed to back Lauren's company, Polo Fashions, Inc. Hilton gave Lauren $50,000 in credit and contracted to manufacture the Polo line of men's wear. With a new deal in the works, it was time for Lauren to leave Beau Brummell. Ned Brower voiced no objections. After all, Polo was only a small fraction of Brower's business. Brower agreed to let Lauren take the name Polo and the Polo trademark (a Polo player on horseback) as his own. In exchange, Brower insisted that Lauren buy the excess inventory—both fabrics and finished ties.

While Lauren began his new job, Joe Aezen sold off the boxes of unsold ties wherever he could. On October 18, 1968, the papers of incorporation for Polo Fashions were filed in New York. Four days later, Lauren showed his first men's suit design to the public and to other established designers, such as Pierre Cardin, Bill Blass, John Weitz, and Oleg Cassini. His suit design was a far cry from the big, baggy sack suits in vogue at the time. In a fashion show at the Plaza Hotel in New York City, Lauren presented a new shaped look—a one-button suit with ultra-wide lapels. Tie-maker Ralph Lauren had become Ralph Lauren, men's wear designer, famous for his English tweedy look adorned with the Polo label.

With the expansion of his business, Lauren needed a place to work. When Polo finally vacated the Empire State Building, Lauren moved to a narrow ten-story residential building in midtown Manhattan just west of Fifth Avenue on Fifty-fifth Street. Fashion designer John Weitz already had his showroom in the building. At his new location, Lauren turned one of the two bedrooms into a showroom, the other his design studio. He delighted in pointing out to visitors that his father Frank Lifshitz had painted his apartment, including putting a faux finish on the fireplace to create an illusion. His offices and location projected the image of Lauren's exclusivity. Over the next twenty years, Lauren slowly purchased the entire building.

Norman Hilton had wanted Lauren to move a little farther downtown to the area known as the garment district, where most men's wear companies had showrooms in one building. But Lauren objected—the garment district was too noisy and too commercial for his tastes. He did not want the Polo name listed in a lobby directory with hundreds of other manufacturers.

Brisk sales of Lauren's ties caused Bloomingdale's to invest in an advertising campaign for the Polo name. On December 7, 1968, Bloomingdale's placed a big, seven-column ad in the *New York Times* that read: "The age of elegance inspires the unique design of our 'Regency' tie by Polo." An oversized illustration of one of Lauren's tapestry ties ran with the text:

> Delving into the past for inspiration, Polo revives the singular design and imaginative colorations of the Regency era for our magnificent tie. Its distinctive geometric pattern and subtle multi-coloring bespeak an age of masculine elegance . . . Done in sumptuous silk from Switzerland, it is handmade and bar tacked at both ends, $15.

As a result of the advertising blitz, Bloomingdale's buyer Gary Shafer—the one who had earlier refused to buy Lauren's ties—saw Bloomingdale's customers buying five and ten at a time, never mind the above-average cost.

About this time, salesman Phil Feiner, Lauren's first employee, resigned. Anthony Edgeworth, then working for

Norman Hilton, replaced him. Edgeworth said, "I was the executive VP . . . My job was to go with Lauren to look at goods and go to the factory in Linden, New Jersey, and try to get the clothing going, but customers came in and I'd have to sell them these ties . . . Business was so incredible, we couldn't make the ties fast enough."

As the business increased, Lauren expanded his staff at his new offices. Understanding the image Polo portrayed was a must for new employees. He hired Steve Krauss, the executive at Bloomingdale's who had by-passed others in order to buy Lauren's ties. Krauss recalled that Lauren would show his ties and suits like they were his children. He would hold his breath, waiting for people's reactions.

Lauren knew little about making suits. He lacked technical skills, such as sketching and pattern making. He knew how he wanted a suit to look, and he was fanatical about details. However, he had no idea of the construction involved in the process from start to finish. His lack of technical skills frustrated Michael Cifarelli, tailor and the head of Hilton's suit factory. Though Cifarelli was known for his fine workmanship, he refused to take orders from an untrained newcomer to the business. One day, Cifarelli bickered with Lauren over the cut of the shoulders of a jacket on a factory dummy. Then, Cifarelli jerked the jacket off the dummy and began jumping up and down on it with his feet.

Bickering continued until the first suits shipped to Bloomingdale's, and they were a disaster. The pants were too long. Some of the jackets arrived with sleeve lengths just below the elbow. Merchandise manager Frank Simon sent the entire shipment back. Lauren blamed Hilton and Hilton blamed Lauren. Nobody was happy. Even so, Norman

Hilton wanted the Hilton-Lauren partnership to work. He knew Lauren was talented but needed to broaden his education about men's wear design and manufacturing. Early in 1969, Hilton suggested that Lauren accompany Ed Brandau on a buying trip to Italy. Lauren and Brandau had worked together at Brooks. Now, Brandau worked for Hilton, developing a line of Italian-made pants.

Several weeks later, Brandau went to Lauren's apartment to pick him up for the journey. Lauren got in the car, visibly upset. After a few minutes, he hopped out of the car and went back upstairs. Ricky was pregnant and he did not want to leave. "Finally I convinced him," said Brandau. "It also turned out that he was very frightened of flying, something he told me when he was on the plane." At that time, Lauren had never traveled abroad.

Rome was the first stop. Brandau and Lauren "shopped the stores"—fashion lingo for sniffing out ideas and buying items that can be knocked off or adapted. Lauren continued looking and shopping, even at dinner.

One night, Brandau took Lauren to one of Rome's finest restaurants. Brandau wondered why Lauren kept staring at their waiter, who wore a washable white cotton jacket. After much gesturing, Lauren made it known that he loved the cut of the jacket and bought it off the waiter's back. From Rome, they traveled to Milan, center of high style and fashion. Then Lauren headed farther north to buy fabrics for his suits. They also visited factories and mills in Como, Italy.

Back in New York, Lauren worked with Cifarelli to create a new collection based on the Roman waiter's jacket. Once again, Lauren's project flopped. Customers did not like the deconstructed look, and they did not want their jackets to look like shirts. Although the jackets failed, they were two decades ahead of their time.

Despite his fashion mistakes and the ups and downs of his first year in men's wear, Lauren still believed in his revolutionary ideas. The spring of 1969 was a happy time for Lauren and Ricky. They moved from the Bronx to an apartment on Manhattan's Upper East Side. On May 7, their first child, Andrew, was born.

Soon, Lauren met Leo Lozzi, a master tailor. Lozzi was a partner in Lanham Clothes, a manufacturer of men's wear in Lawrence, Massachusetts, when the two met. In mid-July 1970, Lauren moved the production of his men's wear line from the Hilton factory to the Lanham factory. Norman Hilton, who owned half of Polo Fashions, was against the move, but Lauren insisted. Lauren's relationship with Hilton had followed a similar path as his relationships with both A. Rivetz & Co. and Ned Brower at Beau Brummell. At the time, Lauren was still a somewhat bungling businessman, who wanted recognition more than money.

Like Michael Cifarelli, Leo Lozzi had also been born in Italy. Whereas Cifarelli was rigid and unbending, Leo Lozzi tuned in to Lauren's ideas. Lozzi said, "Ralph wanted a garment to look such a way . . . he made gestures with his hands . . . rounder, softer, a longer lapel, high pockets . . . he makes the motion and you have to understand the motion. I understood what Lauren wanted."

Soon after beginning to work with Lozzi, Lauren stunned the fashion world by winning the Coty Award for best men's wear designer of 1970. After all, Lauren had been in business for not quite two years. The award, created by Coty Cosmetics in 1943 was one of the premiere honors in the

Models at a late 1960s fashion show in Italy. (*Courtesy of AP Images*)

clothing industry. Prior to 1969, the Coty Award was given only to designers of women's fashions. Bill Blass was the recipient of the first Coty for men's wear in 1969.

Winning the Coty Award thrust Lauren into the top rank of American designers. Fashion editor Buffy Birrittella of the *Daily News Record* wrote major stories about him, raising awareness of his designs. Winning the Coty also gave Lauren an edge in persuading Bloomingdale's to open a Ralph Lauren shop within the store. Ties still accounted for more than half of his company's sales volume. But Lauren wanted to showcase his entire collection—ties, sportswear, raincoats, shirts, and suits—together in one space. He told Frank Simon at Bloomingdale's that he needed his own shop because he was selling a lifestyle. In his uncompromising way, Lauren threatened to go elsewhere if he did not get his own shop.

For the second time in his brief career, Lauren had come up against Bloomingdale's—and won. In the fall of 1971, the Ralph Lauren Polo Shop opened on the north side of Bloomingdale's main selling floor and looked just as Lauren wanted—classy but not stuffy. Marvin Traub, president of Bloomingdale's, recalled, "He not only wanted a shop, he wanted a very expensive one. Parquet floors, wormy chestnut wood, and a lot of leather." The concept of selling a lifestyle worked. Shoppers who intended to buy only a tie or a shirt ended up buying an entire outfit. Despite some criticisms, the men's shop, although a brand new idea at the time, was a great success.

In addition to the opening of the Ralph Lauren Shop in Bloomingdale's, another major event for the Laurens occurred in the fall of 1971. On October 3, David, their second son, was born. Due to their increasing family size, the Laurens

The Ralph Lauren section of Bloomingdale's in 1979 *(Courtesy of AP Images/Dave Pickoff)*

moved from their one-bedroom apartment to a two-bedroom in the same building on the fashionable Upper East Side of New York City.

Lauren and Ricky loved being active with their children. Much time was spent outdoors enjoying sports with their boys. Unlike many of their friends, they preferred family activities over participating in the New York night life, such as society parties.

Lauren in the 1970s *(Courtesy of Susan Wood/Getty Images)*

Lauren and Ricky standing with their sons Andrew (left) and David in 1995. *(Courtesy of DMI/Time Life Pictures/Getty Images)*

"My father always played the role of a regular father . . . he was always there for dinner so we shared a lot of our youth with him . . . My memory of my dad is not of a guy who was famous but the person whom I wrestled with and ran around with when I was a kid," Andrew recalled.

David Lauren remembers that his "dad very rarely talked about business problems but he educated us from when we were little about everything he was doing . . . We had very serious debates."

At age thirty-two, Lauren was a success. He had a beautiful young family, and he owned half of a company that brought in $4 million a year. Now that he was making money, he treated himself to a silver Mercedes sedan.

But Lauren would soon learn that money could roll out as fast as it rolled in.

FIVE

Financial Storm Clouds

Soon after Ralph Lauren's shop opened in Bloomingdale's, Jerry Magnin of Beverly Hills, California, begged for the chance to open a Polo boutique on Rodeo Drive near his own men's specialty store. No one had ever offered to open a Ralph Lauren store before. And no American designer of men's wear had his own freestanding boutique at that time.

But Polo had a problem. Back in the days when Lauren did business from his tiny office in the Empire State building, he had granted exclusive rights to sell Polo Fashions in Beverly Hills to Berny Schwartz. It was an easy thing to do since no one else wanted them. However, Schwartz had never committed to establishing the Polo image because he was more interested in showcasing his own line of suits. In the end, Lauren decided that the deal with Magnin was too big of an opportunity to turn down. So, loyalty aside, Schwartz had to go.

The entrance to Lauren's Rodeo Drive store *(Courtesy of Rodolfo Arpia/Alamy)*

The Rodeo Drive store opened in the fall of 1971. Lauren had a say in the design and furnishings of the building, and the hiring of the manager and salesmen. In the first few months of operation the store suffered from lack of stock. However, this problem pushed Lauren to design new items, such as shoes, belts, and sweaters, to fill the empty shelves. Despite the stock and delivery problems, the Rodeo Drive Store, as Jerry Magnin promised, added status to Polo's image.

The success of his men's wear business boosted Lauren's ambition to expand his business. Since beginning his own line of ties, he shared wife Ricky's frustration at not being able to find the kind of clothes she wanted. Lauren said, "We used to spend Saturdays doing all the stores, and we nearly always ended up depressed and frustrated because

An assortment of Ralph Lauren Polo shirts. *(Courtesy of Frances M. Roberts/Alamy)*

there was nothing we wanted to buy." At the urging of his supporters and admirers, he eagerly moved into the women's wear market.

His timing was good. Beginning in the 1930s, American stores looked to Paris for inspiration and adapted French designs to ready-to-wear women's fashion. Seventh Avenue also offered watered-down versions of the Paris look. By the 1970s, many New York fashion firms that had relied on Paris were gone. Department stores had closed their millinery and high-end fashion departments in favor of boutiques. There was a strong movement to design clothes that a broad spectrum of women in the United States would buy and wear. The transition in fashion from the old order to fashion designs that reflected the American way of life coincided with Lauren's decision to enter the women's market.

Well-known women's fashion designers, such as Bill Blass and Pierre Cardin, often moved to men's wear. People in the industry thought women shoppers would never buy women's fashions from a men's wear designer. According to Polo salesman Ken Giordano, "You might say there was a lot of skepticism, because until then designers had first established themselves in the women's business and then moved into men's wear. We were doing the opposite. And there were a lot of things we didn't know . . ."

Back then, Lauren did not know how to design women's clothing. But he did know what appealed to his wife Ricky. He loved the way Ricky looked on the weekends, wearing one of his shirts. Ricky has always been an important influence on Lauren. He credits his wife with being his toughest critic.

True to his nature, Lauren's venture into the women's fashion world had to be different from other designers.

Models wearing Lauren's women's designs in 1986. *(Courtesy of AP Images/Richard Drew)*

There was already a huge business in women's blouses in the early 1970s. Designer Anne Klein and others made blouses that were feminine and soft for the older fashion-conscious woman. But man-tailored shirts as a fashion item for women did not exist. So, Lauren launched his women's wear collection with shirts. Lauren had found a gap in the market. As Marvin Traub of Bloomingdale's pointed out, Lauren was "moving in a new direction. In fact, he'd uncovered a new retailing opportunity." More than anything else, he presented his new line in such a way that gave it instant distinction.

The label in his women's shirts read "Polo by Ralph Lauren." To compete in the women's business, Lauren knew he needed a more personal label than the label inside his men's wear that read "Polo Fashions." Also, by using his own name, Lauren identified himself as a designer.

On the shirt cuff Lauren placed a polo player—barely an inch long—for "that little touch, like a piece of jewelry." This was the first time Lauren used the polo insignia on his clothing. "The polo player became the new status symbol for women," said Bloomingdale's buyer Raleigh Glassberg. A woman wearing a Ralph Lauren shirt communicated an image of sophistication and style. As it turned out, the addition of the polo player logo was a stroke of genius.

In the beginning, Lauren used high-quality fabrics—cotton, linen, and silk—all from his stockroom to make the women's shirts. The shirts were made like a man's shirt, from the fabrics to the stitching. They looked like a man's shirt with a trim fit, high under the arms. All the shirts were in bold colors, solids, and stripes—and all had white collars and cuffs, adorned by a polo player. Lauren had the shirts

Lauren's polo insignia *(Courtesy of Alamy)*

made in his Polo shirt factory in Mount Vernon, north of New York City.

Buffy Birrittella, former reporter for the *Daily News Record,* was an early recruit to Lauren's new venture. She served as Lauren's publicist and executive vice-president of women's design and advertising. Although hired as Lauren's press person, Buffy soon became "a jack of all trades, assisting him in everything."

In the early days, instead of hiring a professional model, Lauren used Buffy Birrittella as a model for his women's samples. Buffy looked a lot like Ricky, petite and trim. To Lauren's satisfaction, his new line of slim shirts with skinny arms looked great on Ricky. But there was a problem. Most women did not look like Buffy or Ricky. However, this did not stop women from wanting the shirts. If they could not button the shirts or the sleeves were too short, women bought one size larger or more than their usual size. Wearing a shirt with a polo player became chic.

Bloomingdale's carried the first women's shirts made by Lauren. Response was overwhelming. Despite the fact that they were much more expensive than similar items in the store, the shirts sold out immediately. It was obvious that if the merchandise was desirable enough, size and price was only a minor consideration. Since the shirts were an instant hit, Bloomingdale's opened another store within the store for Ralph Lauren's women shirts. His new little shirt bar was on the third floor, near the escalators—for all to see.

To boost Christmas sales even more, Bloomingdale's decided to run a big ad in the *New York Times* on December 12, 1971. The copy read: "Polo by Ralph Lauren for the girls . . . it's that fabulous man's world shirt . . . stripes, thoroughbred solids . . . collared and cuffed in white . . . all wearing the symbolic polo player on the cuff . . . 6-16, $24."

The success of his shirts encouraged Lauren to do a full women's collection. Bloomingdale's championed the idea. Less than ten months after Lauren's initial venture into shirts, the Ralph Lauren shop for women's wear opened on the third floor of Bloomingdale's alongside the big European fashion names of the time; Lauren's shop was across from Yves Saint Laurent's.

In May 1972, Lauren showed his first women's collection. He had scaled down his men's line to a woman's proportions. The collection included a brown Harris Tweed suit with slim sleeves and a tapered waist, and a gray flannel suit with a high waist and cuffed pants. Also in the collection were blazers, pleated pants, and shirts. For the times, all of the designs in his women's collection were brand new.

The *New York Times* took note: "With all the talk about classics, someone was bound to bring back the mannish tailored suit. Fortunately, it was Ralph Lauren who knows something about tailored." This was at the time when career women wanted to dress with as much authority as men. Lauren offered women in the business world a professional wardrobe that was stylish and reasonable in price.

In the early '70s, young people rebelled against the establishment in various ways. A woman wearing a man-tailored suit was an "acceptable way to express a sophisticated brand of nonconformism." Again, Lauren proved to be in tune with the culture of the time.

Nothing in his men's wear business had prepared Lauren for the frenzied pace of women's wear. He was both designing and manufacturing his women's clothes. In contrast to spring and fall collections in men's wear, women's wear had a spring collection, a summer collection, a fall collection, and a winter resort collection. Every collection meant new styles, new fabrics, and new colors. It was chaotic and nonstop. Lauren's days consisted of meetings, brainstorming, choosing fabrics, attending fittings, and hiring more people. Then, when it seemed impossible to add one more thing, Bloomingdale told Lauren he had to start designing a second line of moderate-priced men's wear pants because Polo knockoffs had become big business at half the price of Lauren's products. Although knockoffs were standard operating procedure in the garment industry, Lauren was furious. His answer to the polo knockoffs was Chaps, a subsidiary that sold men's wear at lower prices. Lauren created Chaps because it made business sense and because that was what the stores wanted. But Polo would always be first in his heart.

In 1972, Lauren introduced his signature logo polo knit shirt. Although he was not the first designer to do so, his shirt was different. He used soft 100 percent cotton for the shirt. And instead of using a limited range of colors, Lauren made his shirts in thirty bold colors. Polo knit shirts were an instant success—and a new American classic.

Despite its success, Lauren's company was experiencing growing pains. From its earliest days, Polo had problems with manufacturing and shipping on time. Expansion into the demanding area of women's wear increased delivery delays. In addition, Lauren's financial problems mounted. The Chaps line was selling, but also causing additional cash-flow problems. In a small cash-strapped company, too much growth means danger. More sales means more debt for piece goods, including interest and repayment of the principal. Knowing how fast to expand and how much risk to take became a critical issue for Polo. Lauren realized that he lacked the business and financial skills to manage his rapidly growing operation.

Again, Lauren turned to an old friend from the Bronx neighborhood, Michael Bernstein, for help in solving his problems. Bernstein, a certified public accountant, joined Polo in 1971 as treasurer of the company. In addition to managing the company's finances, his job included overseeing the staff, watching the sales, and analyzing piece goods purchases. Bernstein worked hard to straighten out the company without much cooperation from members of the staff who resented taking orders from a newcomer.

Even so, throughout 1972, Polo remained a company out of control. Bankers were concerned about the high return of unsold, Polo garments because of late deliveries. Collecting payments from boutique owners plagued the company. Finding new banks to loan money to Polo was another problem. The firm failed to pay on time the federal withholding taxes for its two hundred employees that year and had to pay penalties for the late payments.

Despite his lack of cash, Lauren bought out his partner, Norman Hilton. In December 1972, Lauren became the sole owner of Polo Fashions. Negotiations had been underway for a year. Lauren agreed to pay Hilton $633,000 for his half of the firm. Lauren had to borrow $150,000 to make his first payment to Hilton.

As a fashion designer, 1972 was a banner year for Lauren. He received good reviews on his men's wear. His women's collection wowed both retailers and customers. Financially, however, the year was a nightmare. Sales for January and February lagged because contractors demanded cash payments before manufacturing and shipping merchandise. As a result, Polo's volume of sales was $340,000 less than projected, and sales were behind $125,000 at Chaps. The financial situation looked bleak.

Lauren did not let his financial woes interfere with his spring fashion show. Lauren's fall collection of men's wear went on as scheduled. His optimism showed in the fall line. *New York Times* reporter Anne-Marie Schiro wrote, "The words he uses to describe his fall collection are 'dapper,' 'neat,' and 'traditional'. . . What really embodies the spirit of polo '73 is an outfit Lauren calls the 'Vanderbilt'. . . You just know the gentleman wearing it belongs to a private club . . ."

In March of 1973, Polo Fashions was on the verge of bankruptcy, despite a new factor: John P. Maguire, Inc. bought Polo's outstanding bank debt and took over as Lauren's lender. It was risky. But on paper, the projections made by Bernstein seemed plausible. Maguire's account executive, Dave Goldberg, knew Polo had problems. But he viewed them as manageable problems. Goldberg outlined a plan to put the company on a sound financial footing: bring in qualified accountants; establish tighter controls; cut the overhead; and make changes to the manufacturing process.

Goldberg did not like what he found on Polo's books. He said that the financial statement "wasn't a valid picture of the financial condition of the company." Goldberg drew up a new financial statement for Polo. He showed Lauren that despite sales increases, Polo Fashion had no cash, and it owed debts of more than a half million dollars. The news visibly stunned Lauren. But what really shocked Lauren was Bernstein's astonishment at the losses—since he was the one responsible for financing, credit obligations, and cash flow.

A few days later, J. P. Maguire informed Lauren that further financing depended on Polo meeting five demands. The first thing Lauren had to do was turn over his personal passbook savings of $80,000 to Maguire. This meant that the cash in the account was earmarked for Maguire and could not be attached by any other debtors. He also had to renegotiate some of his old debts as well as renegotiate the terms of his buyout deal with Norman Hilton. Then he was told to license out both Chaps and the struggling women's wear division—that is rent his name to others who would manufacture and market the products and pay Lauren a fee. Finally, Goldberg said that Lauren had to ask for prepayments from big accounts like Bloomingdale's.

It was at that moment that Lauren realized that he was close to losing everything—his company and his personal assets. He said, "it wasn't bankruptcy, but it was scary. I had to reorganize the company. I was living in the middle of a panic and I was in pain. But somehow I felt I wasn't going out of business and that it was going to be all right."

SIX

License or Go Under

I n early June of 1973, Ralph Lauren walked into the office of his longtime friend, Michael Bernstein, and fired him. "He was in charge," Lauren reasoned. "He had the financial role and I trusted him . . . He was over his head and he didn't tell me."

Bernstein was the first to go as Lauren took steps to save his company from bankruptcy. He persuaded his brother, Lenny, to join Polo as vice-president and manager, a new position, and he hired Harvey Hellmann, chief financial officer of a big jeans company, to help Lenny untangle the bookkeeping and production snarls. Still looking for people he felt he could trust, Lauren also brought in his other brother, Jerry Lauren, who became vice-president of design, also a new post. Jerry left his job as a design director at a boy's clothing manufacture to take the position.

Lauren with his brother, Lenny *(Courtesy of J. Vespa/WireImage)*

Lauren was under tremendous pressure to jump-start his company. In an effort to comply with J. P. Maguire's demands, he met with Marvin Traub of Bloomingdale's to ask for an advance on the Polo goods that Bloomingdale's had ordered for fall. Without an advance, Lauren would not be able to buy fabrics to make the garments—or make his payroll. Traub agreed to the unprecedented request. But Bloomingdale's concession was only a stop-gap solution to Lauren's larger financial problems. The big drain came from manufacturing his women's line. "What he needed to do was pump cash into the business and license the manufacturing of his women's line," Traub recognized. "However, Ralph had never licensed anything, and was afraid of losing control of his name."

In the midst of all his financial worries, Lauren continued to excel as a designer, winning a second Coty Award for men's wear. And like it or not, he realized that licensing was a necessity, so in October 1973 he signed a ten-year licensing deal for his women's wear with the Kreisler Group. Under the terms of the agreement, Polo would receive $250,000 as a licensing fee, plus 5 to 7 percent of yearly sales. Lauren continued designing. But the Kreisler Group took care of everything else. They bought the piece goods, hired contractors, manufactured the garments, and shipped the finished product. These actions fulfilled two of Goldberg's mandates for Polo: it licensed-out part of the business, and it gave Lauren capital to invest. It wasn't easy going, but Lauren's company showed signs of recovery.

Before 1973, the name Ralph Lauren meant little to the general public, despite his two Coty Awards and the store on Rodeo Drive. He had found "a niche in the market, but no way to get the exposure he wanted." Then in the midst of his financial troubles, he found "a way to flesh out his image on a larger screen."

In 1973, a film company offered Lauren a commission to make some of the men's clothes for a new movie version of F. Scott Fitzgerald's novel, *The Great Gatsby* set in the 1920s. This was a dream assignment for Lauren, who had been enthralled with movies since his boyhood. For his earliest men's wear designs, Lauren had turned to the clothes

A scene from the 1974 film, *The Great Gatsby* (Courtesy of ZUMA Movie Stills Library)

of the Jazz Age for details—collars, ties, and suits without vents. Lauren could not contain his excitement and began telling the world about his good fortune. The fashion media hopped on the bandwagon, crediting Lauren as the film's men's wear designer. The truth of the matter was that the company hired Lauren as the provider of the men's wardrobes—not as a designer. Nonetheless, the clothes looked as though they came from Lauren's showroom, and the label in every jacket read Polo.

Theoni Aldredge was the film's costume designer. The press releases infuriated her. Aldredge blamed Lauren for stealing her limelight. Just before the film opened in 1974, Aldredge called the studio, threatening to sue if Lauren's name was not removed from the credits. The studio refused. But she got her revenge. In her acceptance speech for winning an Oscar for costume designer for the film, she thanked the director and the producer of *The Great Gatsby* with no mention of Lauren. From Aldredge's speech, no one would ever have known that Lauren had had anything to do with the film. But no matter, the publicity and the exposure increased the sales of Polo. "*Gatsby* was a great moment for Lauren because it gave him the kind of recognition outside the industry that he had been seeking," recalled a Polo employee. Lauren liked being in the limelight and seeing his name in print.

Later, Lauren would take credit for designing the costumes for the movie *Annie Hall*. Again his critics emphasized that he did not specifically design a wardrobe for the star, Diane Keaton. However, she did wear some of Lauren's designs in the film.

Dave Goldberg liked the way business at Polo Fashions had started to improve. The financial plan to pay off Polo's debts showed signs of working. Norman Hilton agreed to a longer payout schedule for the debt owed by Lauren. Goldberg had reason to believe that the worst was over for Polo and the company was on the road to recovery. But J. P. Maguire disagreed and sent Lauren a notice that Maguire's financial backing would be withdrawn in sixty days.

Instead of this being the death blow for the company that some expected, the United Virginia Factoring Company took over the account. As it turned out, this was Polo's last major financial hurdle. Polo continued to operate with its overhead reduced and paying creditors on time. The licensing out of Chaps men's wear reduced costs further.

"By making our payments when we promised, we started to build credibility," said Harvey Hellmann. "And for the fiscal year ending March 31, 1974, we showed a profit." This meant that Ralph Lauren could now buy fabrics on credit.

With the company making a profit, Lauren bought another car, and Ricky was pregnant again. They moved into a three-bedroom apartment before their last child was born. In May 1974, a daughter they named Dylan was born.

In the summer of 1974, Lauren won his third Coty Award, this time for women's wear. Lauren was as surprised as everyone else in the industry. After all, Lauren had been making women's clothes for only two years.

That fall Lauren persuaded Peter Strom to join Polo. Strom would run the business, and Lauren would concentrate on design. Lauren met Peter Strom back in 1968. At that time, Strom worked for Norman Hilton. It was Strom who hammered out the deal that persuaded Hilton to become a partner with Lauren. Strom was also involved in the negotiations when Hilton sold his interest in Polo to Lauren. Throughout his financial troubles, Lauren sought Peter Strom's advice. Lauren believed that Strom, with his background in manufacturing and understanding of production schedules, was the right man for the job.

Peter Strom proved to be good for Polo. He limited distribution to keep Polo from losing its air of exclusivity. He cut off a large number of accounts, keeping the best and insisting on better presentation in each store. After three months on the job, Strom had fired most of Lauren's staff—including brother Lenny—and brought in his own people. The bill paying improved. And so did the deliveries.

Also, by fall of 1976, Polo's licensees included the Fifth Avenue jeweler Tiffany & Company, a fur maker, a shoemaker, a Japanese men's clothier, and an eyeglass frame maker. The only segment of Lauren's growing business that he owned himself was Polo men's clothing. Everything else was licensed out and manufactured by other companies. Polo's sales, including sales of licensed products, were about $18 million in 1976.

Over the years, Lauren had been approached on a number of occasions to lend his name to a perfume. But Lauren had no interest in being one line of a company, he wanted his own brand. Lauren was well aware that "fragrance was a pure image business . . . and an extraordinary promotional tool for a designer's other products, as well as a source of big volume and windfall profits." In October 1976, Lauren signed what would be one of the most lucrative licensing deals on Seventh Avenue. Marvin Traub viewed fragrance as "the conduit through which Lauren was finally able to communicate his vision to a mass public."

By agreeing to put his name on a line of perfume, Lauren followed a history of fashion designers whose names appear on fragrances. French designer Coco Chanel was the first, with her Chanel No. 5 in the 1920s.

Corporate giant Warner Communications created a new division, Warner/Lauren Limited, to sell and market Lauren's fragrances—Polo for men and Lauren for women. The company owned the rights to Lauren's fragrance names. However, without investing one cent of his own money, Lauren or his heirs would receive royalties for as long as the products were sold.

Lauren knew nothing about how perfumes were made—but he did know how to market a product and promote an image, or so he thought. He insisted that the design for his Polo fragrance resemble a drinking flask, and he wanted the Lauren bottles modeled after his collection of Victorian ink wells. And he had to have the two fragrances tied together by capping the bottles with the same gold doorknob top.

Creating a crystal container to hold a fragrance should be an easy task—but not when Lauren insisted that the bottles have the same sharp corners as on his inkwells. No American glassmaker would undertake the task. Finally, a glassmaker in Spain took on the job. Making the bottles overseas raised the retail price, but Lauren had his distinctive red bottles with sharp edges. The women's perfume bottle reads "Lauren by Ralph Lauren."

For Polo, Lauren chose a simple design—a gold polo player silk-screened onto green glass. By law, each bottle must be identified by a batch number. Lauren thought the number on the bottle would give a cluttered look—so the number went on the bottom. The word Polo never appears on the men's fragrances. A polo player identifies the fragrance.

It took fifteen months and an incredible amount of money to produce the fragrances. "In freewheeling movieland style, the money has flowed. The production and start-up costs for this venture have to rival any in the fragrance industry," wrote Steve Ginsberg in *Women's Wear Daily*. Bloomingdale's in New York City launched Lauren's fragrances—Polo and Lauren—on March 13, 1978. Brisk sales of both perfumes indicated the launch was a success. Not long after the launch, however, the Polo bottles started to explode. This first occurred during the production of a training tape for sales people. Employee Jill Resnick, known in the industry as "The Nose" for her ability to pick winning fragrances, explained on tape the sales points of the products. "Then I picked up a bottle of Polo," she said, "and it exploded. The green ran all over my dress. I was a mess."

Head of operations Oriel Raphael quickly understood. To his horror, lights from the training film caused the bottle to

Lauren in his office in 1978 *(Photo by Edgar de Evia. Reprinted with permission from David McJonathan)*

burst. Soon caps began popping in department stores across the country where Polo was displayed under hot spotlights. Later Raphael discovered that the factory responsible for filling the bottles had stored the fragrances outside in the cold. Excessive heat caused the fragrance to expand so rapidly that it popped off the tops.

The Lauren fragrance also had its share of woes. It turned out that if the red color on the Lauren bottles did not seal completely, it would peel off. Oriel Raphael eventually found a glass factory that fixed the problem.

Lauren launched other scents and a line of cosmetics over the years. Some were successful; others were eventually discontinued. These were minor setbacks, though: all in all, the fragrance licensing business proved profitable for Lauren. By 1987, royalties paid to Lauren from worldwide sales of all Ralph Lauren fragrances amounted to 6.25 million dollars.

Flush with profits from his many licenses, Lauren stood ready to expand into new areas that he had never before had the time or money to tackle.

SEVEN

Riding High

Ralph Lauren's newfound confidence and sharp instincts about his customers showed in his 1978 fall women's wear collection. Lauren's models marched out wearing a wild mix of western looks to the sounds of "Back in the Saddle Again." They wore fringed leather jackets over long prairie skirts, chamois blouses, satin cowboy blouses, satin jeans, and belts with glittering silver buckles. Lauren's relaxed look was hugely successful.

"Lauren Steals the Show," headlined the *New York Times*. That collection influenced retailers and women who were ready for something fresh. It also showed that if Ralph Lauren liked something, he did it—no matter the fashion in Paris or Milan. Lauren explained, "America was my inspiration. Activities of life, not the activities of fashion. I was making that life exciting and working with it. That's what I ignited: American sportswear."

Lauren took advantage of the popularity of the western look by forming a new company, Polo Westernwear, with The Gap. Based in California, The Gap provided the funding and put the production in place to attract customers who buy moderate-priced clothes. In reality, the Gap became a Ralph Lauren licensee. Despite industry predictions of success, the deal was a fiasco. There were so many shipping, production, and fit problems that The Gap lost money. In February 1980, The Gap dissolved its business relationship with Ralph Lauren. A few months later, The Gap announced a $6 million tax write-off against its 1979 earnings.

However, Ralph Lauren did not lose his interest in the western look. A vacation trip to New Mexico with his wife and children became the basis of his groundbreaking Santa Fe Collection. The collection included chamois skirts and turquoise hoop earrings, turquoise prairie skirt, and white cotton petticoat. Navaho blankets and native art inspired the knit wool sweaters. The Santa Fe look was in: it was so popular that knock-offs appeared immediately.

For his next collection of women's wear, Lauren changed direction. For fall 1982, cowboy Ralph Lauren turned to romance. The collection featured Victorian high-necked, lacy blouses and long skirts. Ralph called his trendsetting collection "the beginning of romantic clothes . . . It was very Old World and inspired by Old World appeal." Again, Ralph proved to be in tune with what appealed to his customers. The lacy, antique look was a runway hit.

As his wealth and influence increased, Lauren became the target of attacks.

When the Santa Fe collection hit stores in August 1982, Susan Lydon, writing in the *Village Voice*, accused Ralph of "plundering the nation's treasures for his own personal gain . . . Lauren doesn't merely adapt or revive, he appropriates whole looks and passes them off as his own."

Two months later, England's BBC aired a television show criticizing Lauren for running a sweatshop operation. The show accused Lauren of selling $400 sweaters made by British hand-knitters who earned a meager $10 to $20 a garment.

Despite his critics, Lauren continued to expand his business. It was in the early eighties that Lauren first decided that home furnishings would be his next move. Many of his admirers, appalled by his decision, said, "You're not going to do sheets and things like that!"

That is just what Lauren did, and more. Just as the industrial designers of the 1920s designed products that affected

A room set up to display items from Lauren's Home Collection for fall, 1986. *(Courtesy of Dirck Halstead/Time & Life Pictures/Getty Images)*

everyday life, Lauren created a new lifestyle that had far-reaching effects. "Ralph was the first designer to take his whole design concept from apparel into a full-blown home collection. Remember, we didn't just do tablewear or sheets, or bathwear, we also did lifestyles within those categories," Buffy Birrittella explained.

Lauren introduced his home furnishings line as the Ralph Lauren Home Collection in September 1983. This was the first time that a major apparel designer had moved into home furnishings. The J. P. Stevens Company, maker of sheets and towels, agreed to manufacture Lauren-designed sheets, pillowcases, comforters, and towels. Others were licensed to make glassware, silverware, china, and wall coverings. Ralph insisted on launching the household products—2,500-piece collection—all at the same time in major department stores across the United States.

In the beginning, the Ralph Lauren Home Collection was plagued by the usual woes of Polo: late deliveries, empty shelves, and irregular merchandise. Peter Strom, Lauren's partner said, "The interest was phenomenal . . . But the marketing was disastrous, the merchandising needed a lot of help, and the production was terrible."

As in the past, Lauren's company had tried to do too much too fast. Clearly, launching all products at once instead of just a few lines the first season was a mistake. Lauren's insistence that each store carrying his line have a special Ralph Lauren Home Collection department was not wise. Decreeing that there would be no seasonal markdown for Lauren's sheets and towels did not help sales either.

"We saw that it wasn't right, and we changed it," said Lauren. In 1984, Lauren took control away from J. P. Stevens, and in 1986 the Ralph Lauren Home Collection became a wholly owned subsidiary of Polo Ralph Lauren. Additionally, he expanded the Home Collection to include furniture. A year later the collection was on firm ground and a success.

The line continued to be so successful that ten years later Lauren became the first designer to put his name on paint. With his name on the product, it had to be as upscale as every other item bearing his name. Advertising campaigns featured the paint can with its Stars and Stripes label and announced sixty-eight Perfect Shades of White, such as polo-mallet white and pocket-watch white.

As he had done with apparel, Ralph Lauren created a variety of looks for his 1986 Home Collection. He divided the collection into four categories: New England (American traditions), Log Cabin (rugged outdoor life), Jamaica (tropical living), and Thoroughbred (English heritage). In traditional Lauren manner, the name of each group conveyed the concept and represented a lifestyle.

Lauren realized that if his clothes and home furnishings projected a lifestyle, his advertisements had to provide glimpses into the world of that lifestyle. Fashion photographer Bruce Weber created many images for Lauren. Weber did his first shoot for Lauren in 1978. By the mid-1980s, he was producing multi-page advertisements—huge location productions running as long as twenty pages in glossy magazines. A shoot for Lauren resembled a film set, as did the ads when they appeared.

Over the years, Lauren dreamed of opening his own store. That dream became a reality in 1986 with the opening of the Polo Ralph Lauren store—the ultimate Polo shop—in the Rhinelander Mansion at 867 Madison Avenue in New York

The Rhinelander Mansion *(Courtesy of Frances Roberts/Alamy)*

City. The Rhinelander was a personal triumph for Lauren. It was the pinnacle of a career that had started many years before in the Bronx, where this son of immigrants wore hand-me-down clothes.

In 1894, wealthy Gertrude Rhinelander Waldo hired architects to build her a home, styled like a French château. Completed five years later, the five-story limestone building featured a ballroom, billiard parlor, and bowling alley. Yet, no one ever lived in it. Gertrude Rhinelander Waldo's husband died during the years of construction, leaving her distraught. After her husband's death, she decided to live with her sister—across the street from the mansion. The Rhinelander Mansion remained entirely vacant until 1921. From that time until Lauren became involved in the project, various commercial tenants had occupied the mansion, leaving it in dire need of restoration.

Renovating the building was a major investment for Polo Ralph Lauren. One advisor did not think the investment was "justified on a risk/reward basis." Naomi Leff, the design consultant on the project, recalled that Lauren passed the Rhinelander on his way to work. She said, "I suppose the idea just grew gently within him. It was a major act of faith but you must never forget that with Ralph Lauren you are dealing with a man with a major vision. People said it was too big . . . It was too small. He would take business away from his existing outlets; it was in the wrong location. Everybody advised against it. The decision was his alone."

With the exception of his men's wear business and the store he bought in London in 1983, Ralph Lauren had never put his own money into new projects. Peter Strom, Lauren's partner said that "thinking about the project and bank loans . . . left him dizzy with anxiety in spite of the company's growth." What made the breathtaking venture even more daring was that Lauren does not own the building—he has a long-term lease. At the time, a group of Saudi Arabian investors owned the property. And since 2005, the Rhinelander Mansion has been owned by Sloan Capital, an Irish investor group. The cost of the two-year renovation project grew to $30 million plus—four times the original estimate.

Ralph Lauren turned his piece of folly into a triumphant success. His achievement was so great that it dwarfed everything else he had done. "This store is everything I ever wanted to say in my life: a total fulfillment. It's not about clothes. It's about elegance and classicism . . . I want this to be an experience for people . . . If they can come in here and have a sense of warmth, like they were in somebody's home, that's what I want to give people."

From its opening day, the Rhinelander has afforded customers a shopping experience like no other—the aura of an English country estate, with a grand staircase, carved ornaments on the ceiling, round arched windows, and merchandise concealed in chests of drawers and English highboys. Cashmeres sweaters flung over a chair's arm, walking canes, and cricket bats, give each room its own distinct personality. Artifacts scattered throughout the store give the effect of an English baronial hall.

According to Marvin Traub, the Rhinelander store came out of the pages of Scott Fitzgerald's 1925 novel, *The Great Gatsby*. "It was fantastic. This was Gatsby's mansion. Every detail was perfectly executed. Vintage tennis rackets and lacrosse sticks rested in rooms as if they'd just been left there a moment ago. When a book was on a shelf, it was a book not a fake binding . . . It was as if the images in Lauren's head had finally become three-dimensional."

A year after its opening, *Women's Wear Daily* claimed the Rhinelander to be one of Manhattan's hottest tourist attractions. The newspaper also reported that the store shattered "expectations for its first year by doing in excess of $30 million, more than triple the pre-opening projection."

True to Ralph Lauren's prediction, rather than take sales away from other New York stores that stocked Polo Ralph Lauren, the Rhinelander stimulated sales at those stores. The astonishing success of the Rhinelander changed fashion retailing all over the world. A smiling Ralph Lauren, not quite forty-seven years old, appeared on the cover of *Time* magazine's September 1, 1986, issue.

Lauren on the cover of *Time* magazine in 1986. *(Courtesy of Dirck Halstead/ Time & Life Pictures/Getty Images)*

Nonetheless, a shadow loomed over his success. A few months after Lauren had been on the cover of *Time*, he met Marvin Traub for lunch. Immediately, Traub sensed something was wrong. "I've just had this cover story in *Time*," Ralph explained. "I'm worth millions, I have all this success. Most people think I should be very happy. But this is a very difficult time for me. My father is in the hospital, I've just been up to see him. My brother had a stroke, and six months ago I was told that I have a brain tumor that's probably benign but needs to be operated on . . ." He went

Lauren looking over ads with his staff in 1986. *(Courtesy of Dirck Halstead/ Time Life Pictures/Getty Images)*

on to tell Traub that he had decided to put off the surgery until after his spring show.

Then, Lauren grabbed Traub's arm and said, "I'm having a terrible headache right now." Traub rushed Lauren to New York Hospital. On April 13, 1987, five days after he showed his fall 1987 collection, Lauren had an operation. Even though the lump was not cancerous, the surgical procedure was extremely dangerous. News of his operation was not announced until three days later when the doctors believed Lauren was out of danger.

Lauren's brain tumor had been a well kept secret. At first, he told only Ricky. Peter Strom was told later. Two weeks later Lauren told his children, still in their teens. "I was so nervous about telling them," he said. "But they were terrific."

By August, Lauren was back in is office, ready to design his upcoming collections. "I went back to work with a much greater fury . . . I don't take anything for granted." He was eager to show the world he was back and better than before.

EIGHT

The World of Ralph Lauren

Ralph Lauren entered the 1990s with good health and a long string of fashion hits. He had gone from selling his signature wide neckties in 1967 to having the first in-store boutique for men in Manhattan's Bloomingdale's. Not only was he the first American designer with his own store on Rodeo Drive in Beverly Hills, but he became the first American designer to open a freestanding store in Europe, on New Bond Street in London. The opening of his lavish flagship store in the Rhinelander Mansion in New York City ranked as his greatest achievement, and Lauren had expanded his evening wear offerings, from floor-length sweaters to strapless ballet-length dresses to full-blown ball gowns. All the while, he continued to borrow styles from the past, freshening them into a new look.

Lauren and other fashion designers offered people a myriad of clothing options in the 1990s. There was much

A Ralph Lauren store on New Bond Street in London, England.
(*Courtesy of Sean Potter/Alamy*)

less adherence to strict fashion rules. No longer did fashion filter down from the aristocracy to the average woman. The runways continued to influence fashion, but other fashion influences came from the streets, from rock and roll, hip hop, films, and television. Women began wearing exercise clothing on the streets, leading to a wide range of casual and leisure wear.

The fashion house that Ralph Lauren and Peter Strom built now generated retail sales in the billions. In the 1990s, Lauren focused on making over the house of Polo. From the beginning, other designers had copied Lauren, taking away market shares. Lauren rival, Calvin Klein, did it with jeans. The Gap came out with "small p" polo shirts. For the most part, lauren appeared disinterested in the other companies. However, Tommy Hilfiger was considered a real threat. He had hired away some key Polo employees. And he was appealing to the young, hip crowd with his cheaper lines. In 1992, Hilfiger's company went public. Soon after, the stock price tripled.

Since other designers had gone to cheaper sports lines, Lauren felt the need to appeal to the sons and daughters of his customers to compete. His first move was to mark down his core product—polo shirts. To reach young shoppers, he added the Polo Sport line of high-performance athletic apparel. In 1993, the Polo Sport store opened in a building across the street from the Rhinelander Mansion. Lauren told the *New York Times*, "The fashion of the nineties is about health. And when I say health, I don't mean doctors. I mean body consciousness, consciousness of eating the right foods, throwing away the junk foods, feeling good on the inside and looking it on the outside."

Models showcasing Lauren's Polo Sport line of clothes. *(Courtesy of AP Images)*

As with all Lauren stores, Polo Sport abounds with props that create a mood. Canoes and kayaks fixed to the white lacquered walls evoke a sense of the outdoors. Suspended from the ceiling is a racing scull. Vintage skiing posters and a bank of video screens bolster a modern, outdoorsy mood. To his critics, Lauren said, "I am moving, I am not sedentary. I do clothes which are authentic and this is my statement."

By 1994, Lauren, now fifty-four, was caring for his dying father. Frank Lifshitz had a heart condition and suffered from dementia, as well as anemia and kidney disease. He had received round-the-clock nursing care since 1990. Then without any warning, Lauren's mother, Freida Lifshitz, had a heart attack and died on February 1, 1994. His father lived only a few more months and died on July 6, 1994.

That summer, Lauren's company experienced financial setbacks again. Cash reserves were low, and Polo was deeply in debt. The failures dimmed Lauren's hopes of buying back his women's operation. His troubles were further compounded by a knockoff dispute that erupted with French designer Yves Saint Laurent. Saint Laurent charged that Lauren's $1,000 sleeveless tuxedo gown was a copy of his $15,000 couture version. A French judge found Lauren guilty and imposed a $411,000 fine. The case was settled with Lauren paying a much lower fine.

Lauren receives applause after presenting one of his fashion collections. *(Courtesy of Jon Levy/AFP/Getty Images)*

In spite of its ups and downs, Polo had remained a solid business. In his efforts to reinvent the company, Lauren eventually bought back his women's fashion license. It was not easy, but he closed the deal in mid-August of 1995. Within twenty-four hours of getting the license back, Lauren turned around and licensed a lower-priced women's line called Lauren. However, he kept the higher end of his women's line in-house.

Still needing to increase sales volume, Lauren signed a license to make jeans. In the past, he had experienced a number of failed attempts in the denim business—the first in 1978 with the Gap Company. This time, the licensee, Sun Apparel of El Paso, Texas, agreed to produce a line of low-cost jeans as well as advertise them and open Polo Jeans stores. While jeans made by Polo Jeans Co. had to be inexpensive ($48 a pair), they also had to "maintain an inspirational, premium-brand status."

By accommodating new ideas and changing as the culture changed, Lauren turned his company around. Worldwide retail sales of Polo Ralph Lauren merchandise neared $5 billion by 1996.

With his financial troubles eased, Ralph Lauren reintroduced his top-of-the-line Purple Label collection of $1,800 men's tailored suits. The exclusive Purple Label was sold only in the best department stores and Polo Shops. A massive ad campaign featured Ralph Lauren and model Tyson Beckford, of Jamaican and Chinese descent, wearing Purple Label suits.

Polo Sport, Purple Label, and Lauren, the new mainstream women's collection, lifted Polo's sales as the fashion company prepared to go public. On Wednesday, June 11, 1997,

Lauren rang the bell to open the New York Stock Exchange. It was now official: Polo Ralph Lauren was a public company. Marvin Traub said that it had not been an easy decision for Ralph Lauren. "He agonized over it. He had great concerns, being a private individual, about the exposure he would have, but at the same time he was convinced that it was the right move to build the business."

Going public with the company helped Lauren expand his interests globally, beyond its stores in Germany, Greece, France, and the Netherlands. By the 1990s, he started the process of buying back some of the estimated 350 licenses under which his products are manufactured, while at the same time opening new stores with distinct atmospheres. In 1998, for instance, the company spent $200 million to buy back the license for the two-story, mahogany-paneled Ralph Lauren store in Paris at the intersection of Rue Royale and Place de la Madeleine. This is one of the busiest areas of the city in terms of pedestrian and street traffic. Nearby are other famous designer stores, including Mario Valentino and Karl Lagerfeld.

Then in May 1999, Ralph Lauren opened a new store in London to replace his original store, and he opened a second, bigger store on the same street.

Ralph Lauren's quest to expand and create new styles has continued unabated. In 2001, Lauren's son, David, became senior vice-president of marketing, advertising, and corporate communications of Polo Ralph Lauren, and in 2004, under David's direction, Polo launched Rugby, a preppy lifestyle collection geared to college students.

Lauren's most recent moves have been to expand his luxury business in Japan and the Pacific Rim. The largest

Ralph Lauren store in the world opened in Tokyo in March 2006, and in the same year he signed a five-year agreement to outfit the on-court officials at the U. S. Open tennis tournament at Wimbledon. The Tokyo store is 24,000-square-feet, with a Beaux Arts-inspired facade, and marble staircases, Ottoman limestone columns, and Persian rugs inside. "I'm not designing clothes," Lauren once remarked. "I'm creating a world."

In 2007, Lauren opened a store in the birthplace of his parents, Russia. It was his second, and this newest store occupies three stories of a major corner on Tretyakovsky Passage, which in terms of prominence and stature is similar to Los Angeles' Rodeo Drive. Lauren's cultivated, classic American styles were well received there. On opening day of Tretyakovsky Passage, the store reportedly sold seventeen Ralph Lauren Ricky bags. The handbags, made of American alligator and fitted with custom-made Italian hardware, carry price tags of up to $14,000.

In February 2008, J. C. Penney launched its American Living line, a new moderately priced clothing and home furnishings line created by Ralph Lauren. Though supplied by Polo Ralph Lauren, American Living's forty categories of merchandise will not carry the Polo brand's horse. Instead, the logo is an eagle and a flag.

When he's not focused on business, Lauren finds time to pursue other passions and interests, such as collecting vintage automobiles, acquiring and decorating new residences, and contributing to charities. His personal automobile collection includes a yellow 1937 Alfa Romeo, a 1929 Bentley race car, a 1955 Mercedes 300SL Gull Wing Coupe, a 1965 Aston Martin DB5 Volante, several Porches, Jaguars,

Ferraris, and a red Maserati. In 2004, the Boston Museum of Fine Arts displayed sixteen of his cars in an exhibit titled "Speed, Style, and Beauty." As for his homes, Lauren owns a Norman-style manor house that sits on 250 acres of lawn and rolling hills in Bedford, a city about an hour north of Manhattan; a Manhattan townhouse overlooking Central Park; a beach house in Montauk, New York; a seaside villa in Jamaica; and the sprawling 16,000-acre Double RL Ranch in Telluride, Colorado.

In terms of charities, Lauren and his wife, Ricky, who works as a therapist and counselor, have contributed to the

Lauren's 1938 Bugatti Type 57SC Atlantic Coupe on display at the Boston Museum of Fine Arts. *(Courtesy of AP Images/Steven Senne)*

fight against cancer by establishing the Ralph Lauren Center for Cancer Care and Prevention to serve the Harlem area of New York City. And within days of the terrorist attacks on the United States on September 11, 2001, the Polo Ralph Lauren Foundation set up the American Heroes Fund. The $4-million fund helped various charities in the aftermath of the disaster, including scholarships for children of the victims.

The following year, 2002, the couple launched the Ralph and Ricky Lauren Center for the Performing Arts at the Lexington School for the Deaf, also in New York City, with a gift of $2 million. But Polo Ralph Lauren's greatest gift to charity has been the donation of $13 million to the Smithsonian's National Museum of History for the preservation of the original Star Spangled Banner. "The flag is an inspiration for all Americans and it captures the dreams and imaginations of men and women all over the world," Lauren has said. "I am a product of the American dream and the flag is its symbol."

If anyone knows how to turn a dream in to a reality, it is Ralph Lauren. From his humble beginnings, growing up in a four-room apartment in the Bronx, Lauren has attained his youthful dream of becoming a millionaire many times over. He never attended design school and doesn't sketch, yet his influence as a fashion designer is felt around the globe. He started out in the 1960s selling neckties and today heads a $13.5-billion publicly traded business that produces men's wear, women's wear, sportswear, children's wear, home collections, eyeglasses, fragrances, and even paint. In 1981, he became the first American designer to open a freestanding store in Europe, on London's Bond Street. And with more than 14,000 employees and stores in sixty-five countries,

Lauren stands with President Bill Clinton and First Lady Hillary Clinton during a ceremony to announce Lauren's gift of $13 million for the preservation of the Star Spangled Banner. *(Courtesy of Joyce Naltchayan/AFP/Getty Images)*

his name is universally recognized in the fashion world and beyond.

The Ralph Lauren brand, associated with luxury, old money, privilege, elegance, and style, has earned him the fashion industry's most coveted awards: he is a seven time winner of the Coty Award. In 1992, the Council of Fashion Designers of America presented him with its Lifetime Achievement Award, and in 2007 he won the Council's first-ever title of Fashion Legend because his "vision and innovation epitomizes American design excellence and continues to set the standard of fashion." In 2006 *Time* magazine included him on its list of "one hundred people who shaped our world."

In a 1984, in a five-page magazine ad, Ralph Lauren described the world he was trying to create:

> There is a way of living that has a certain grace and beauty. It is not a constant race for what's next, rather an appreciation of what has come before. There is a respect for the quality recognition of what is truly meaningful. These are the feelings I would like my work to inspire. This is the quality of life I believe in.

It is this "quality of life" that Ralph Lauren has promoted through his designs for more than forty years now—a lifestyle that the public continues to buy.

Ralph Lauren *(Courtesy of Getty Images)*

Timeline

1939   Born in the Bronx, New York City, on October 14.

1957   Graduates from DeWitt Clinton High School.

1962   Serves a stint in the United States Army.

1964   Joins A. Rivetz & Company as a tie salesman; marries Ricky Low-Beer.

1967   Introduces the wide tie under the label Polo.

1968   Begins to design men's wear.

1969   Son Andrew born.

1970   Wins Coty Award for men's wear.

1971   Designs first women's wear collection; first Polo/ Ralph Lauren store opens in Beverly Hills, CA; son David born.

1974   Assists in designing clothes for the movie *The Great Gatsby*; daughter Dylan born.

1975   Receives the American Fashion Award.

1976   Wins Coty Award for women's wear; saves his company from bankruptcy by signing lucrative licensing deals.

1978	Launches Western look for men and women; licenses Ralph Lauren name for fragrances; introduces boy's wear line.
1981	Introduces girl's wear line; opens store in London on Bond Street.
1982	Launches entire collection of home products.
1986	Opens Rhinelander Mansion flagship store in New York City; Polo store opens in Paris.
1987	Undergoes operation to remove benign brain tumor.
1992	Earns the Council of Fashion Designers of America Lifetime Achievement Award.
1994	Makes global commitments to support breast cancer campaigns.
1997	Polo Ralph Lauren becomes a publicly traded company on the New York Stock Exchange.
1998	Gives $13 million for the Save America's Treasures Campaign to preserve the Star Spangled Banner.
2000	Establishes the Ralph Lauren Center for Cancer Care and Prevention in East Harlem, New York.
2001	Is inducted into the first Fashion Walk of Fame 2002; sets up the American Heroes Fund after the World Trade Center attack on September 11, 2001; the Ralph and Rickey Lauren Center for

the Performing Arts at Lexington School for the Deaf in New York City opens.

2005   The Museum of Fine Arts in Boston, Massachusetts, unveils an exhibition of Ralph Lauren's collection of vintage sports cars.

2006   Launches Ralph Lauren store in Tokyo; makes *Time* magazine's list of "The People Who Shape Our World."

2007   Receives a special honor, the first American Fashion Legend Award, from the CFDA (Council of Fashion Designers of America).

2008   J. C. Penney launches its American Living line, a new moderately priced clothing and home furnishing line created by Lauren.

Sources

CHAPTER ONE: Childhood Dreams

p. 12, "like it lived," Michael Gross, *Genuine Authentic: The Real Life of Ralph Lauren* (New York: HarperCollins, 2003), 67.

p. 12, "Ralph would show up . . . " Colin McDowell, *Ralph Lauren: The Man, the Vision, the Style* (London: Octopus Publishing Group Limited, 2002), 17.

p. 13-14, "The clothes went . . . " Jeffrey A. Trachtenberg, *Ralph Lauren: The Man Behind the Mystique* (Boston: Little, Brown and Company, 1988), 23.

p. 14, "be rich," Gross, *Genuine Authentic*, 32

p. 14, "I was not a kid . . . " Ibid., 53.

p. 16, "A waiter was the lowlife . . ." Trachtenberg, *Ralph Lauren*, 27.

p. 16, "I started nowhere . . . " Ibid.

p. 17, "Kids would laugh . . . " Gross, *Genuine Authentic*, 73.

CHAPTER TWO: A Passion for Clothes

p. 19, "A lot of people I met . . ." Gross, *Genuine Authentic*, 76.

p. 19, "It was tough . . ." Ibid., 77.

p. 19, "a really great education . . ." Oprah Winfrey, "Oprah Talks to Ralph Lauren," *O, The Oprah Magazine*, October 2002, 288.

p. 19, "nobody would hire . . . " Gross, *Genuine Authentic*, 83.

p. 19-20, "[Ralph] was responsible . . ." Ibid.

p. 21, "You have no face . . ." Ibid., 85.

p. 21, "My job was . . ." McDowell, *Ralph Lauren*, 19.

p. 21, "Basically, I was selling . . ." Trachtenberg, *Ralph Lauren*, 31.

p. 22, "like the skin . . ." Gross, *Genuine Authentic*, 86.

p. 22, "He had a tendency . . ." Trachtenberg, *Ralph Lauren*, 32.

p. 22, "He liked the . . ." Gross, *Genuine Authentic*, 86.

p. 23, "He pulls up . . . outer space," Ibid., 88.

p. 24, "a season's jump . . ." Ibid.

p. 24, "Abe understood me . . ." Trachtenberg, *Ralph Lauren*, 34.

p. 24, "Somebody will steal . . ." Ibid.

p. 24-25, "She was very European . . ." Gross, *Genuine Authentic*, 91.

p. 25, "European, the Beatles . . ." Trachtenberg, *Ralph Lauren*, 35.

p. 25, "He actually dressed . . ." McDowell, *Ralph Lauren*, 21.

CHAPTER THREE: The Wide Tie

p. 27, "The world is not ready . . ." Gross, *Genuine Authentic*, 95.

p. 27, "There's no such thing . . ." Trachtenberg, *Ralph Lauren*, 36.

p. 29-30, "I know you have. . . "." McDowell, *Ralph Lauren*, 27.

p. 30, "They were all handmade . . . " Ibid., 43.

p. 30, "The ties I wanted . . ." Ibid.

p. 30, "I could not call . . . "Gross, *Genuine Authentic,* 101.

p. 31, "an international quality . . ." Ibid.

p. 31, "They gave me a tiny . . ." Trachtenberg, *Ralph Lauren*, 45.

p. 32, "I couldn't make any . . ." Ibid., 46

p. 32, "The store gives the . . . Gross, *Genuine Authentic*, 105.

p. 33, "Wearing a Ralph Lauren . . ." Trachtenberg, *Ralph Lauren*, 51.

p. 33, "It was fabulous . . ." Gross, *Genuine Authentic*, 106.

p. 33, "At the time . . ." Winfrey, "Oprah Talks to Ralph Lauren," 221.

p. 34, "Aezen as in . . ." Trachtenberg, *Ralph Lauren*, 49.

p. 34, "Frank Simon and me . . ." Ibid., 50.

p. 35, "Gary, I'm dying . . ." Winfrey, "Oprah Talks to Ralph Lauren," 221.

p. 35, "It was like . . ." Gross, *Genuine Authentic*, 107.

p. 35, "I saw a young man . . ." Ibid.

p. 36, "After we put Lauren's . . ." Trachtenberg, *Ralph Lauren*, 54.

p. 36, "prices were crazy . . ." Ibid.

p. 36, "to straighten his cases . . ." Marvin Traub, *Like No Other Store: The Bloomingdale Legend* (New York: Random House, 1993), 210.

p. 36, "My long-range wish . . ." Trachtenberg, *Ralph Lauren*, 56.

CHAPTER FOUR: Founding a Fashion Empire
p. 37, "All of a sudden . . ." Gross, *Genuine Authentic*, 113.
p. 37, "Brower didn't get . . ." Ibid., 112.
p. 38, "people who were . . ." Ibid.
p. 38, "Pete, go find out . . ." Trachtenberg, *Ralph Lauren*, 57.
p. 40, "The age of elegance . . ." Trachtenberg, *Ralph Lauren*, 60.
p. 40, "Delving into the past . . ." Ibid.
p. 41, "I was the executive . . ." Gross, *Genuine Authentic*, 118.
p. 42, "Finally, I convinced him . . ." Trachtenberg, *Ralph Lauren*, 65.
p. 43, "Ralph wanted a garment . . ." Ibid, 66-67.
p. 45, "He not only wanted . . ." Gross, *Genuine Authentic*, 126.
p. 48, "My father always played . . ." McDowell, *Ralph Lauren*, 145-146.

CHAPTER FIVE: Financial Storm Clouds
p. 52, "We used to spend . . ." "McDowell, *Ralph Lauren,* 28.
p. 53, "You might say . . ." Trachtenberg, *Ralph Lauren*, 92.
p. 55, "moving in a new . . ." McDowell, *Ralph Lauren*, 31.
p. 55, "that little touch . . ." Ibid.
p. 55, "The polo player . . ." Trachtenberg, *Ralph Lauren*, 91.
p. 57, "a jack of all trades . . . Gross, *Genuine Authentic*, 130.
p. 57-58, "Polo by Ralph Lauren . . ." McDowell, *Ralph Lauren*, 31.
p. 58, "With all the talk . . ." Trachtenberg, *Ralph Lauren*, 96.

p. 58, "acceptable way . . ." Traub, *Like No Other Store*, 214.
p. 61, "The words he uses . . ." Trachtenberg, *Ralph Lauren*, 127-128.
p. 61, "wasn't a valid picture . . ." Gross, *Genuine Authentic*, 141.
p. 62, "it wasn't bankruptcy . . ." Ibid., 144.

CHAPTER SIX: License or Go Under
p. 63, "He was in charge . . ." Gross, *Genuine Authentic*, 146.
p. 65, "What he needed to do . . ." Traub, *Like No Other Store,* 116.
p. 65, "a niche in . . ." Ibid., 218.
p. 65, "a way to flesh out . . ." Ibid.
p. 65, "*Gatsby* was a great . . ." McDowell, *Ralph Lauren*, 47.
p. 68, "By making our payments . . ." Trachtenberg, *Ralph Lauren*, 152.
p. 69, "fragrance was a pure . . ." Gross, *Genuine Authentic*, 172.
p. 69, "the conduit through . . ." Traub, *Like No Other Store*, 219.
p. 71, "In freewheeling movieland . . ." Trachtenberg, *Ralph Lauren*, 175.
p. 71, "Then I picked up a bottle of . . ." Ibid., 176

CHAPTER SEVEN: Riding High
p. 73, "Lauren Steals the Show," Trachtenberg, *Ralph Lauren*, 197.
p. 73, "America was my inspiration . . ." Ibid., 196.
p. 75, "plundering the nation's . . ." Gross, *Genuine Authentic,* 222.

p. 75, "You're not going . . ." McDowell, *Ralph Lauren*, 97.

p. 76, "Ralph was the first . . ." Ibid. 98.

p. 76, "The interest was phenomenal . . ." Trachtenberg, *Ralph Lauren*, 264.

p. 76, "We saw that it wasn't . . ." Gross, *Genuine Authentic*, 230.

p. 79, "justified on a . . ." Trachtenberg, *Ralph Lauren*, 10.

p. 79, "I suppose the idea. . . ." McDowell, *Ralph Lauren*, 138.

p. 79, "thinking about the project . . . ." Trachtenberg, *Ralph Lauren*, 13.

p. 79-80, "This store is everything . . ." McDowell, *Ralph Lauren,* 141.

p. 80, "It was fantastic . . ." Traub, *Like No Other Store*, 224.

p. 80, "expectations for its first year . . ." McDowell, *Ralph Lauren,* 141.

p. 82, "I've just had this . . ." Traub, *Like No Other Store*, 228.

p. 83, "I'm having a terrible . . . Ibid.

p. 83, "I was so nervous . . ." Trachtenberg, *Ralph Lauren*, 238.

p. 83, "I went back to work . . ." Gross, *Genuine Authentic*, 260.

CHAPTER EIGHT: The World of Ralph Lauren

p. 86, "The fashion of the nineties . . ." McDowell, *Ralph Lauren*, 153.

p. 87, "I am moving . . ." Ibid.

p. 89, "maintain an inspirational . . ." Gross, *Genuine Authentic*, 327.

p. 90, "He agonized over it . . ." Ibid., 337.

p. 91, "I'm not designing clothes . . ." Guy Trebay,

"Captain America," *New York Times Magazine*, August 26, 2007.

p. 93, "The flag is an inspiration . . ." McDowell, *Ralph Lauren*, 164.

p. 95, "vision and innovation . . ." "Ralph Lauren Named Fashion Legend," http://www.showbuzz.cbsnews.com/stories/2007/03/13/style_fashion/main2564323.shtml.

p. 95, "There is a way of living . . ." Tom Reichert and Jacqueline Lambiase, eds., *Sex in Consumer Culture: The Erotic Content of Media and Marketing* (Mahwah, N.J.: L. Erlbaum Associates, 2006), 191.

Bibliography

Agins, Teri. *The End of Fashion: How Marketing Changed the Clothing Business Forever.* New York: HarperCollins Publisher, 1999.

Bolino, Monica, ed. *Fashion.* San Diego, California: Greenhaven Press, 2002.

Buxbaum, Gerda, ed. Icons of Fashion: The 20th Century. Munich, New York: Prestel, 1999.

DeJean, Joan. *The Essence of Style.* New York: Free Press, 2005.

Drucker, Stephen. "Ralph Lauren's Bedford Beauty." *Architectural Digest,* November 2004.

Eaton, Phoebe. "Fashion's Number One." *Harper's Bazaar,* March 2006.

Fiori, Pamela. "Planet Ralph." *Town & Country,* October 2002.

Goldstein, Lauren. "Lauren's European Invasion." *Time,* July 23, 2002.

Gross, Michael. *Genuine Authentic: The Real Life of Ralph Lauren*, New York: HarperCollins, 2003.

Husain, Humaira, ed. *Fashion*. London: Hamlyn, 1998.

Kimes, Beverly Rae. *Speed, Style, and Beauty: Cars from the Ralph Lauren Collection*. Boston, MA: Museum of Fine Arts, 2005,

Lacayo, Richard. "The Dream, Ralph Lauren." *Time*, May 8, 2006.

McDowell, Colin. *Fashion Today*. New York: Phaidon Press, Inc., 2000.

McDowell, Colin. *McDowell's Directory of Twentieth Century Fashion*. Englewood Cliffs, NJ: Prentice-Hall, Inc., 1985.

McDowell, Colin. *Ralph Lauren: The man, the vision, the style*. London: Octopus Publishing Group Limited, 2002.

Mendes, Valeria and Amy de la Haye. *20th Century Fashion*. London: Thames & Hudson, 1999.

Milbank, Caroline Reynolds. *New York Fashion: The Evolution of American Style*. New York: Harry N. Abrams, Inc., 1989.

Molotsky, Irvin. *The Flag, the Poet, and the Song: the Story of the Star Spangled Banner*. New York: Dutton, 2001.

Newman, Cathy. *Fashion*. Washington, DC: National Geographic, 2001.

Perschetz, Lois, ed. *W: the Designing Life*. New York: Clarkson N. Potter, Inc., 1987.

Theroux, Paul. "Ralph Lauren: "The Designer's Sprawling Double RL Ranch in Colorado." *Architectural Digest*, November 2002.

Trachtenberg, Jeffrey A. *Ralph Lauren: The Man Behind the Mystique.* Boston: Little, Brown and Company, 1988.

Traub, Marvin. *Like No Other Store: The Bloomingdale Legend.* New York: Random House, 1993.

Weatherly, Myra, ed. *Living in 1920s America.* San Diego, California: Greenhaven Press, 2006.

Winfrey, Oprah. "Oprah Talks to Ralph Lauren." *O, The Oprah Magazine,* October 2002.

Web sites

http://about.polo.com/
Official Ralph Lauren Web site.

http://www.vintageblues.com/history_main.htm
History of fashion in the United States in the 20th century.

index

Business Leaders

Klein, Calvin, 86
Krauss, Steve, 34, 36, 41

Lauren, Andrew (son), 43,
46, 48, *48*, 74, 83
Lauren, David, 45-46, 48,
48, 74, 83, 90
Lauren, Dylan, 68, 74, 83
Lauren, Jerry (brother), 12-
13, 17, 19, 29, 63
Lauren, Ralph, *10*, *26*, *28*, *47*,
48, *64*, *71*, *81*, *82*, *88*,
94, *96*
Birth, 12
Birth of daughter,
Dylan, 68
Birth of son Andrew, 43
Birth of son David, 45
Changes name from
Lifshitz to Lauren, 17
Deaths of parents, 88
First Polo boutique opens
in Los Angeles, 50
Marriage to Ricky
Low-Beer, 25
Starts designing and selling
ties, 30
Wins Coty Award, 43, 65,
68
Lifshitz, Frank (father), 11-
14,17, 26, 29, 40, 82, 87-88
Lifshitz, Frieda (mother), 12-
14, 17, 26, 29, 87-88

Lifshitz, Lenny (brother), 12-
13, 17, 29, 63, *64*, 69
Lifshitz, Sam (grandfather),
11
Lifshitz, Thelma (sister), 12,
17
Low-Beer, Ricky (wife), 24-
26, *26*, 29-30, 35, 42-43,
45-46, *48*, 52-53, 57, 68,
74, 83, 92-93
Lozzi, Leo, 43

Magnin, Jerry, 50, 52
Mantle, Mickey, 14

Rivetz, Abe, 23-24, 26, 27

Scott, Randolph, 14, *15*
Schultz, Jack, 34, 37-38
Schwartz, Berny, 33, 50
Shafer, Gary, 34-35, 40
Simon, Franklin, 34, 37-38,
41, 45
Strom, Peter, 38-39, 68-69, 76,
79, 83, 86

Traub, Marvin, 36, 45, 55,
64, 69, 80, 82-83, 90

Weber, Bruce, 77
Weitz, John, 39